Choosing Joy

Story and photography
by
Nancy Olson

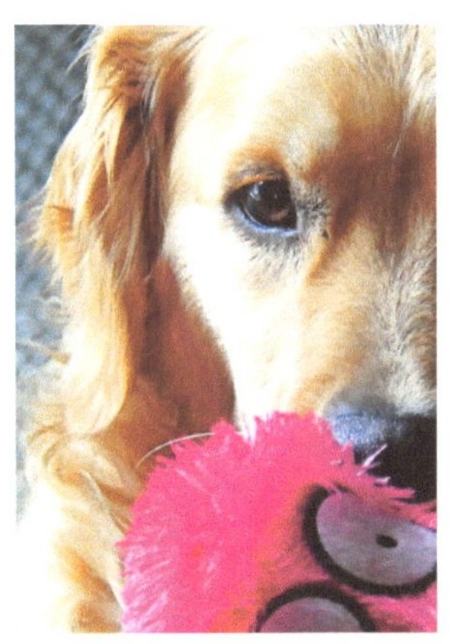
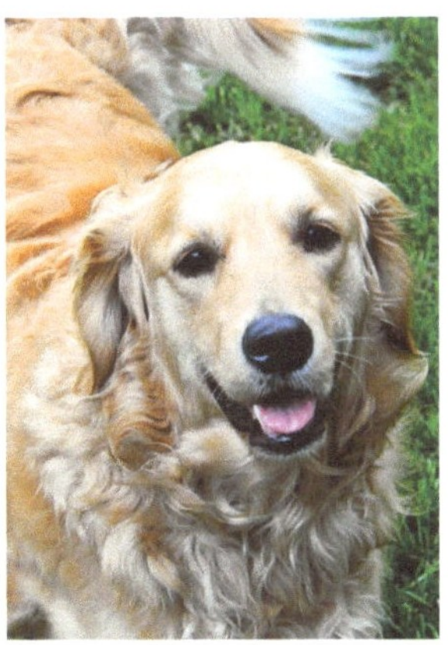
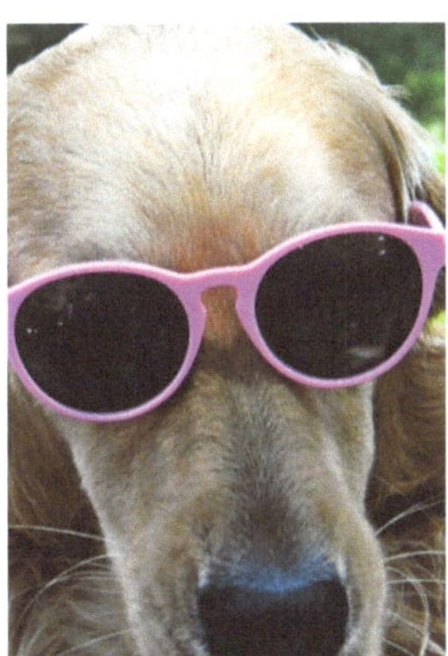
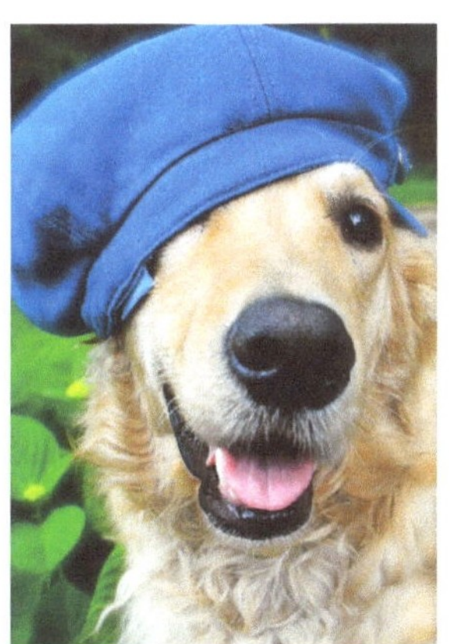

For Augusten

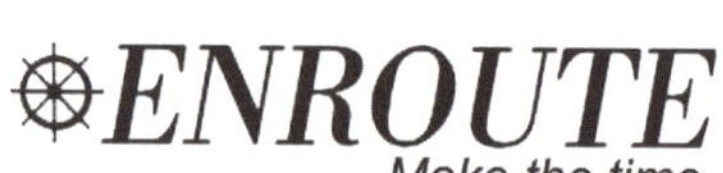

ISBN: 979-8-88870-455-4

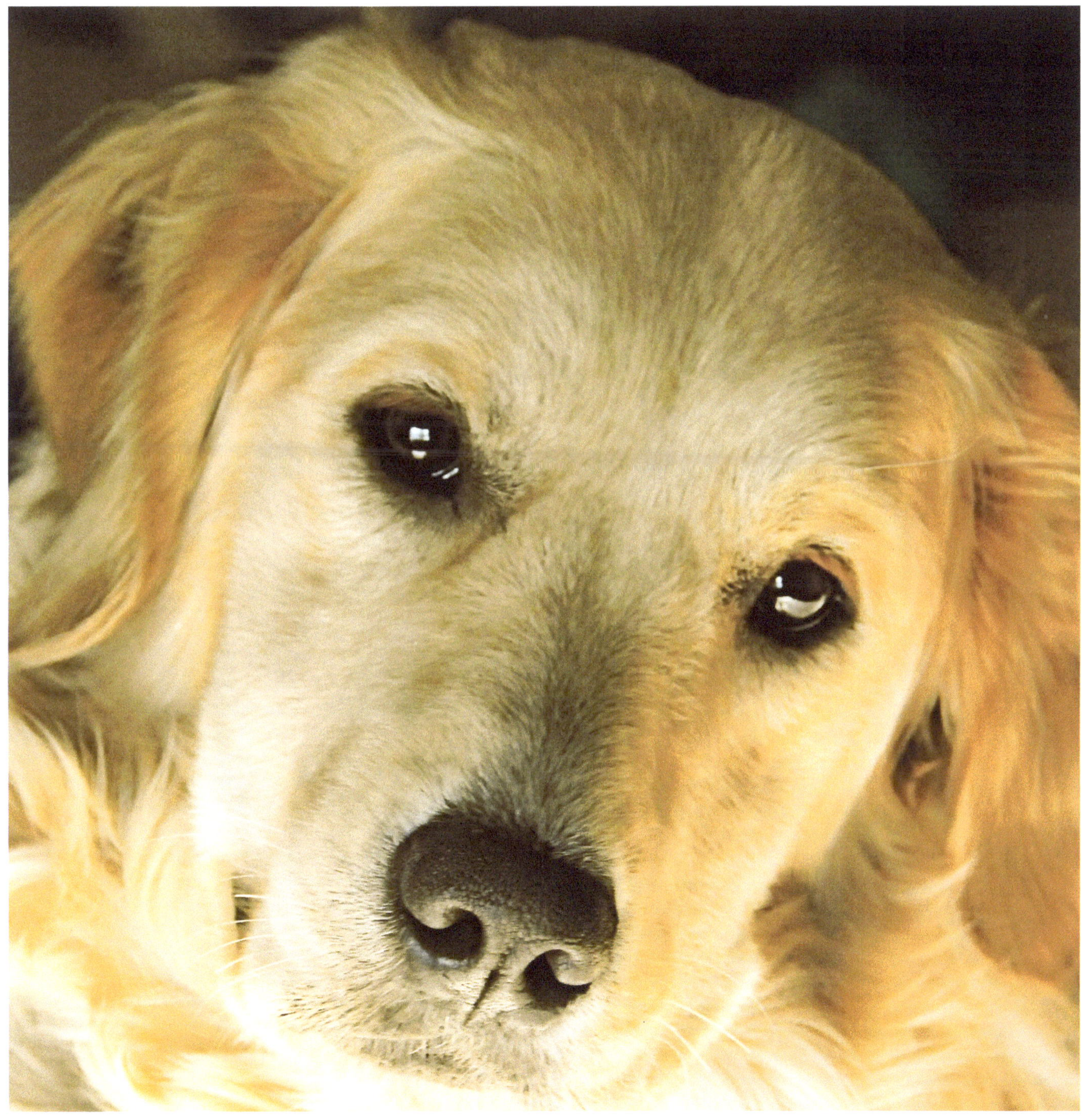

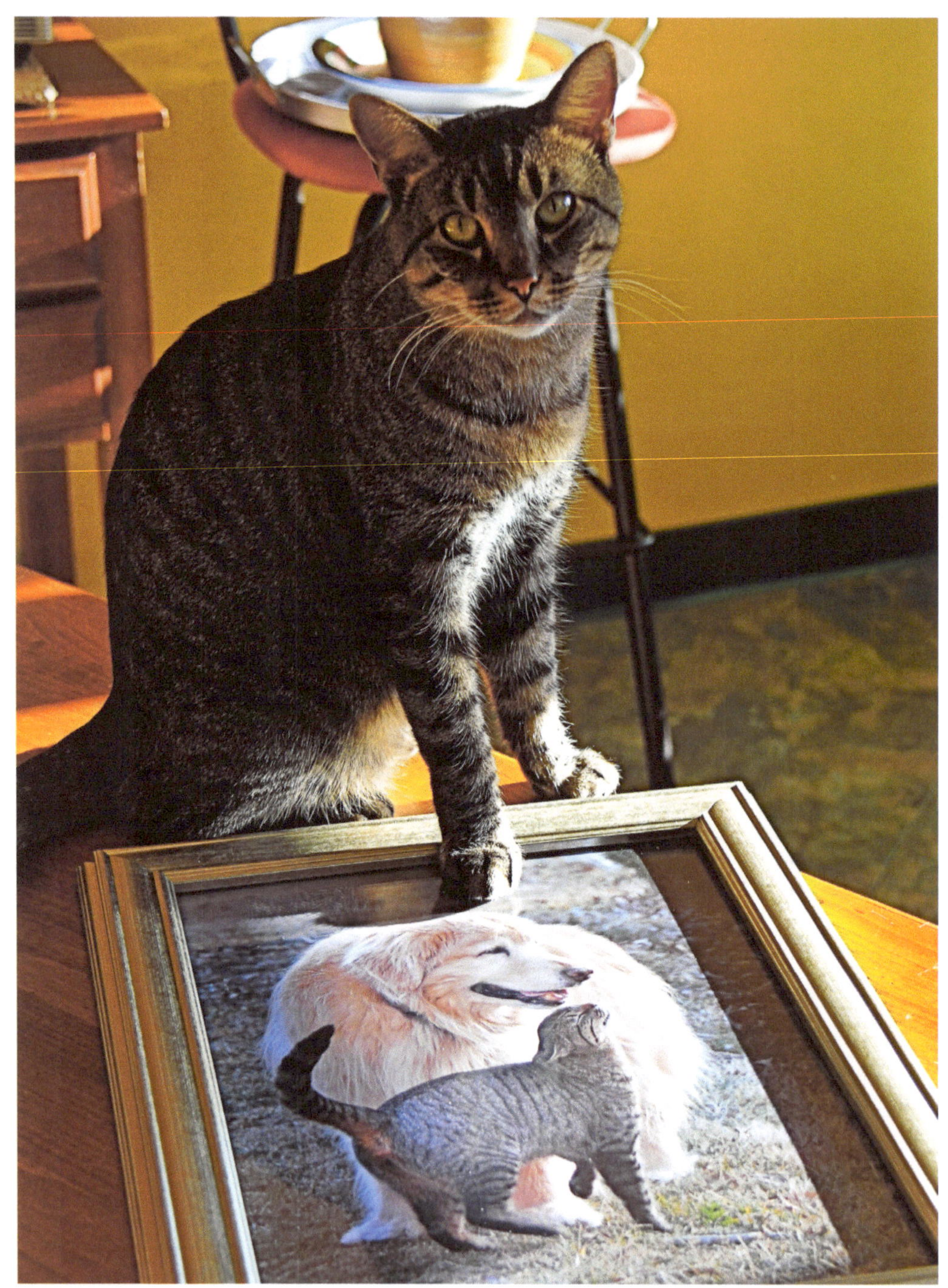

Hunter remembers his friend, Zach.

One fine October morning, all crisp and sunny and bright, we pulled our car into the parking lot of the Golden Retriever rescue facility and parked against the fence. With high hopes, we began our hunt for "the gold."

But maybe I should explain. You see, our family is composed of genuine, card-carrying, dog-lovers. We think that any home without a dog is just a house.

So when our beloved Golden, Zach, passed away, his absence left a lonely void in our home. Even our remaining creature, Hunter the Cat, was lonely without his companion's presence.

So here we were, on the hunt for our next Golden.

Out in the large exercise yard of the adoption facility, we could see a gentleman walking and playing with a small Golden. We stopped awhile to watch. And then . . . she saw us.

In a flash she rushed to the fence and jumped up to get a better look and a little sniff. I think the first words out of my mouth were, "Oh, isn't it wonderful to see a Golden smile again! And what a beautiful face!"

Jeff and I stroked her soft nose through the fence and then spoke to the gentleman.

"Is this pup a female?" we asked.

"Yes, she is a little girl and she is a sweetheart," he replied.

We talked to her a little longer and then we walked away to the front door, entering the adoption center's building.

A friendly woman came to greet us and we remarked about the charm of the dog that had greeted us at the fence.

"Would you like to visit with her?" she asked.

"Well, maybe," we replied. "We have always been partial to male dogs and we would like to look at the boys. We'd love a big, red male."

For the next hour or so, we systematically made our way around the yards, looking at each of the Golden boys, talking to their human helpers, and even taking a couple of them out into the exercise yard to play with us and to determine how they responded.

Some were interested in retrieving balls but not interested in us.

Several had been used as breeding dogs and had not been well socialized with people.

None of them felt just right. And although we wished each one of them well and hoped that each would find a permanent home, it didn't seem that the right home would be our home.

Finally, as an afterthought, we said, "What about the little girl we saw on the way into the building? Can we take her out into the yard?"

Of course we could!

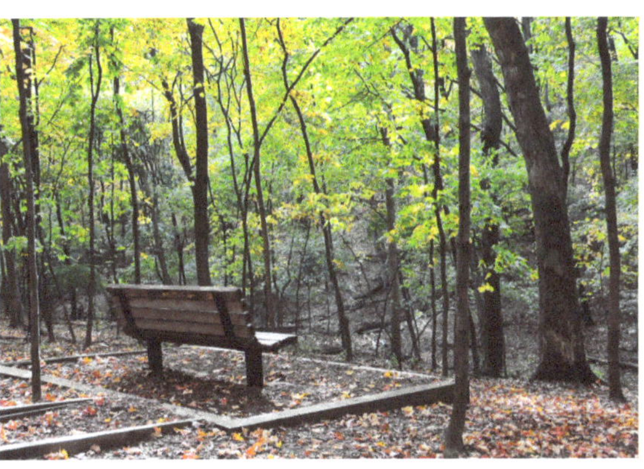

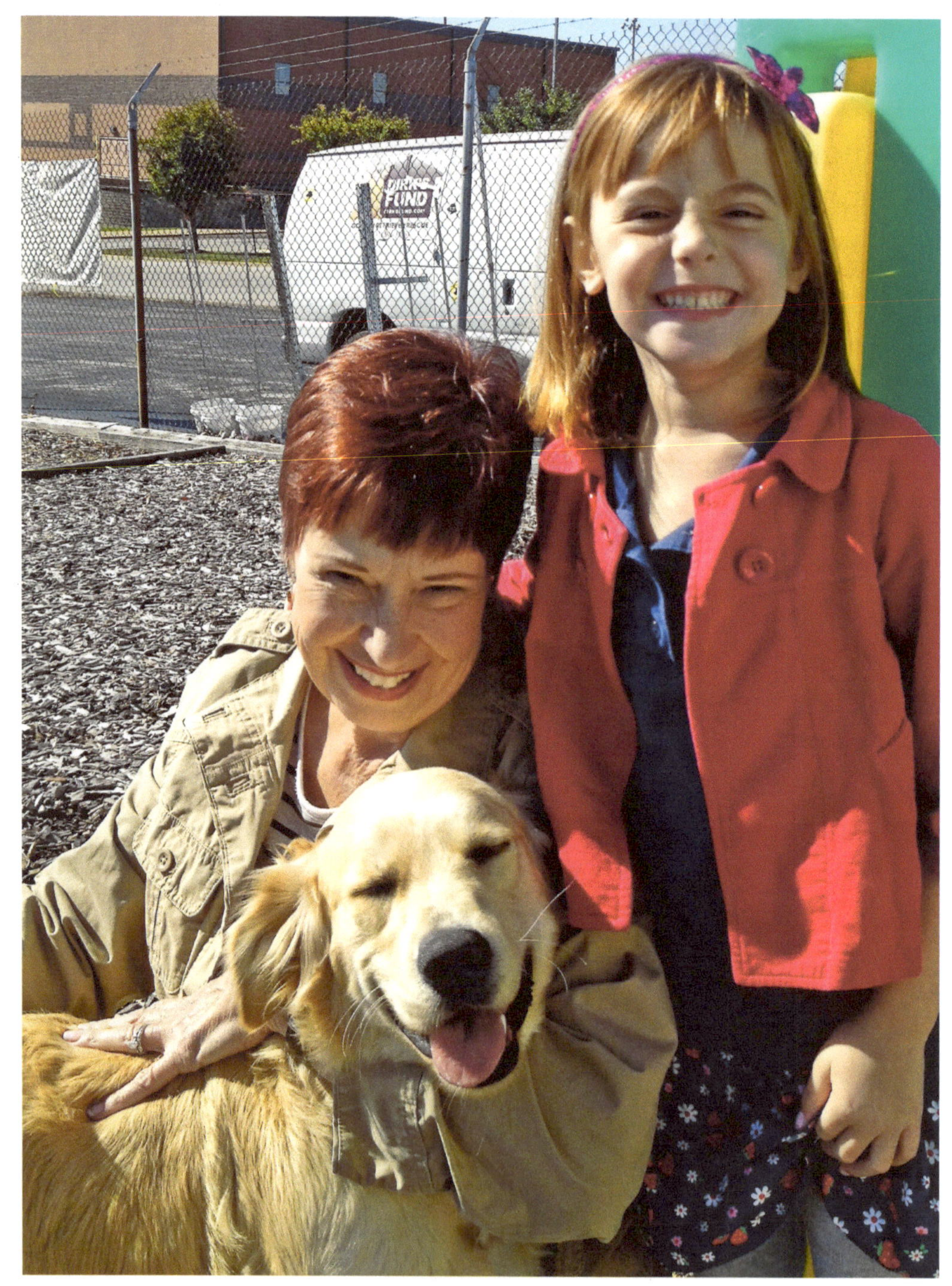

We choose Joy!

By this time, our daughter and granddaughter had also joined us, eager to be with us when we went searching for our new companion.

So out she came, walking on a leash with a handler. As she entered the fenced area, I kneeled down to be on her level. In a flash, she ran to me, jumped up and put her paws on my shoulders, put her nose next to my face, and said, “At last you’ve come! I’ve been waiting for you! Can I go home with you now?” (I’m pretty sure I heard these exact words!)

As my husband took pictures, my daughter said, “That is the most joyful animal I’ve ever seen. You need to adopt her and name her **Joy**.”

And that’s just what we did.

Joy had been right in front of our eyes all along!

But, hold that thought…

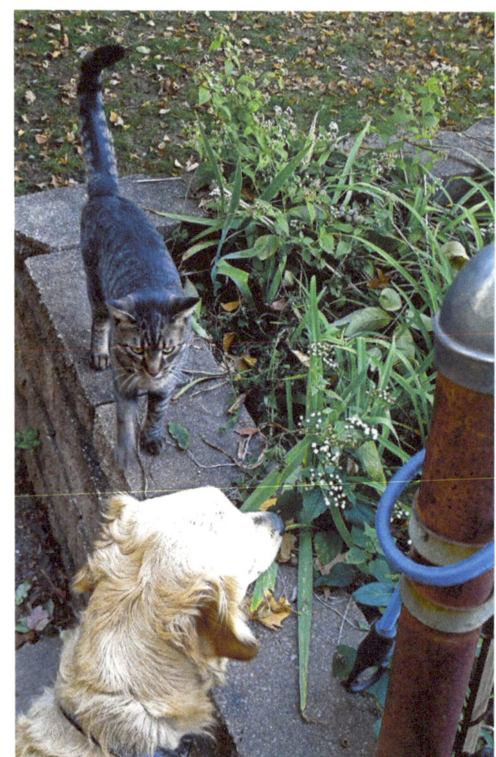
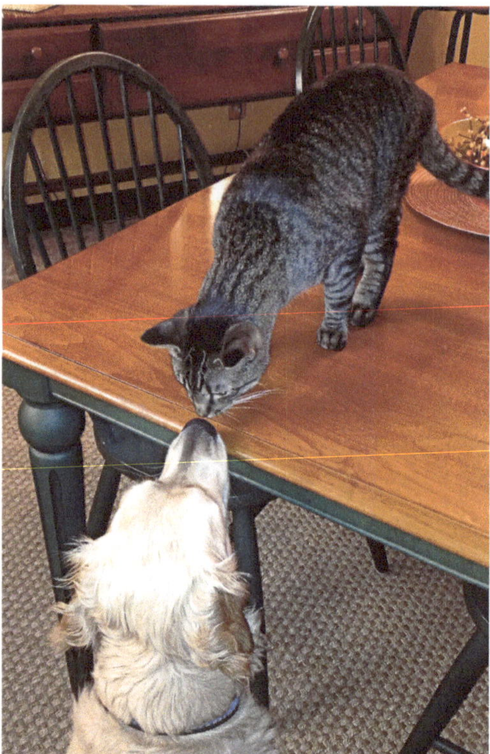
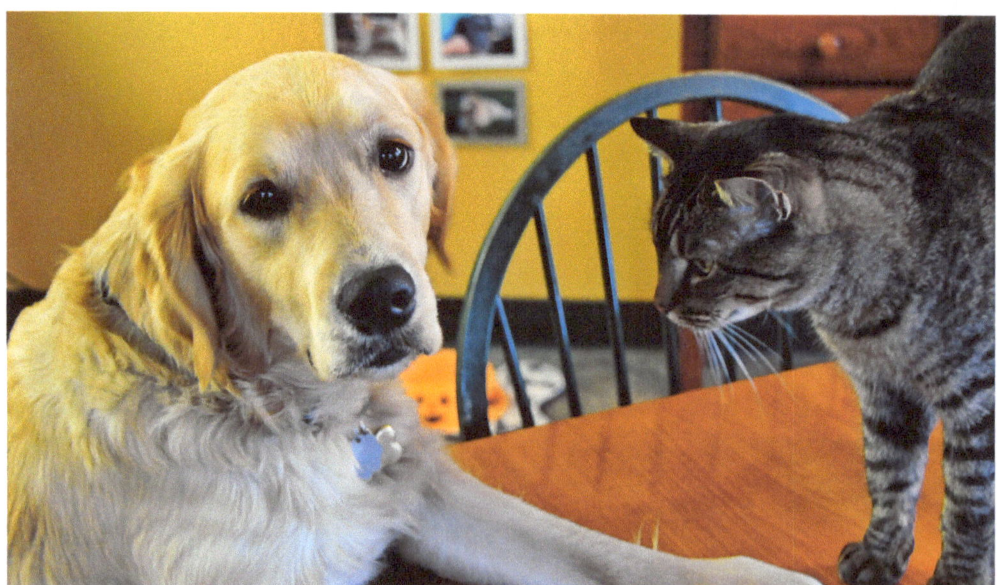

Hunter welcomes a new friend.

When we first began our search for a new Golden companion, I had only two requirements: no chasing the cat and no barking! After their formal introduction and supervised visits for a week or so, Joy and Hunter immediately became great pals.

As for the barking and running requirement . . . Joy passed both tests with flying colors. Actually, Hunter quickly taught Joy how to hunt little critters hidden in the grass, just like he hunts. And as for barking – Joy almost never barks. In fact, we have not heard Joy bark AT ALL in the last year and a half! Prayers answered!

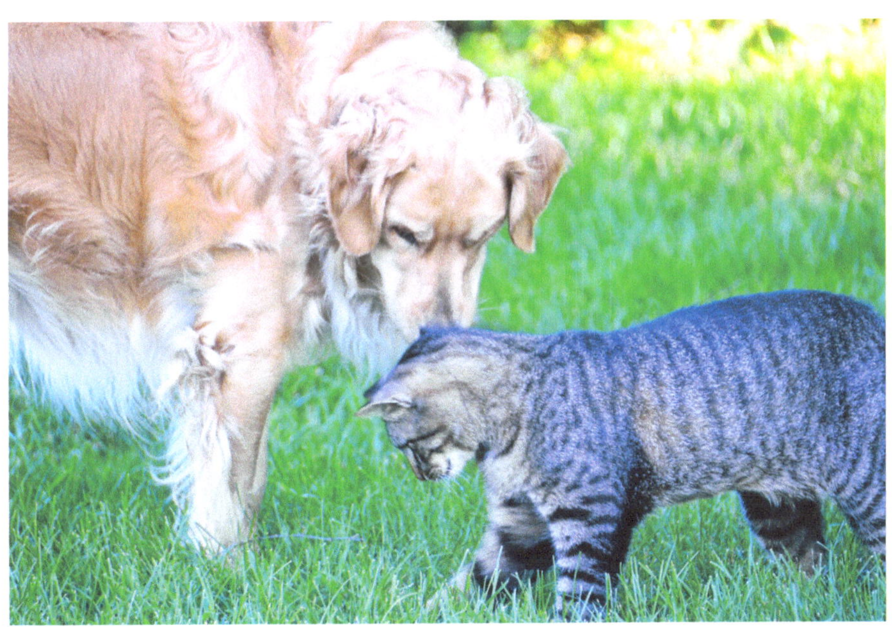

Hunting buddies

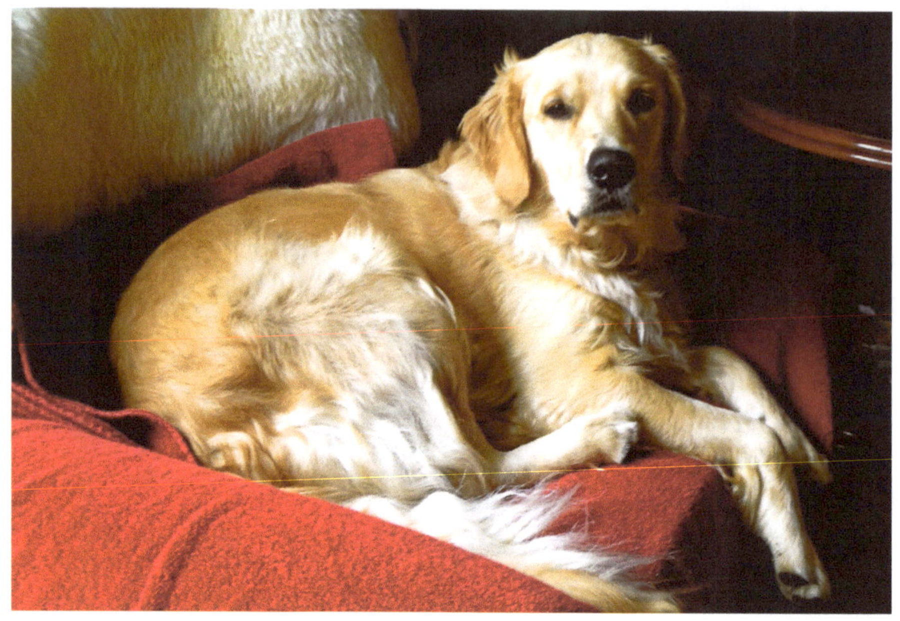

Joy sits upon her throne.

Joy was 16 months old when she came to live with us . . . in many ways still a puppy, but with a previous life that was unknown to us. So she came with some "habits."

After some of the usual adjustments that go with moving to a new home, Joy moved herself right in to her new family. (The correct word here really is "moved.") Right away, she got busy redecorating!

On her second day home, Joy somehow managed to turn around a heavy, upholstered chair in the family room so that it faced us when we watched TV from the sofa. She claimed it as her "throne" and has owned it ever since!

In addition to calling her "Joy," we began to see that her middle name must probably by "Quirky!" Need some examples?

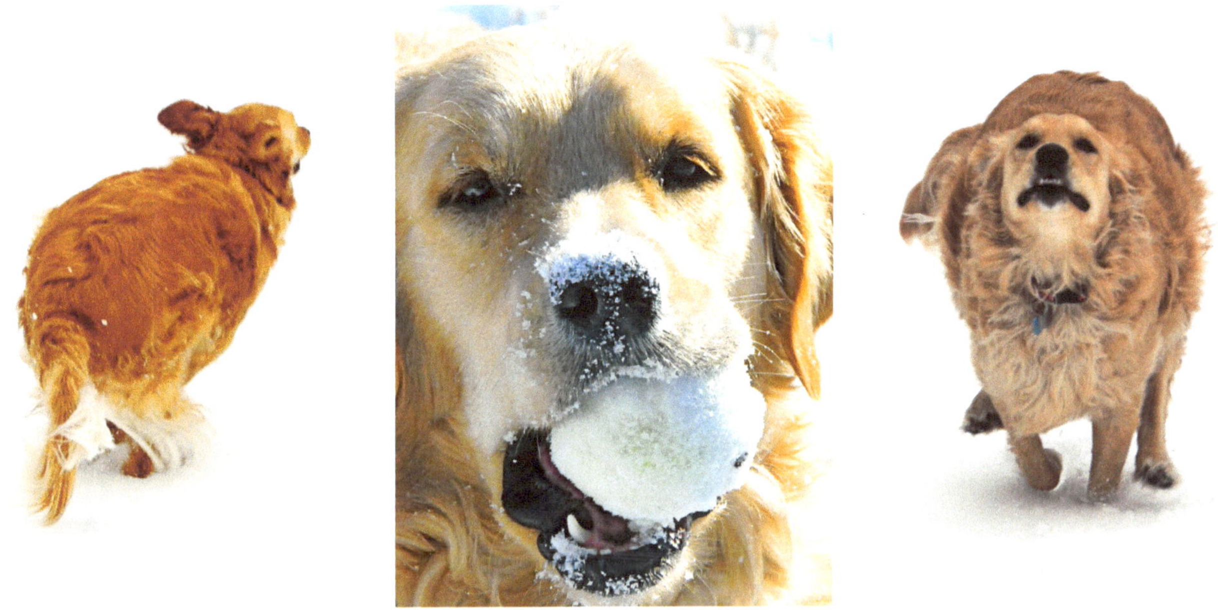

Joy loves the snow so much that she's even convinced Hunter to come out and play.

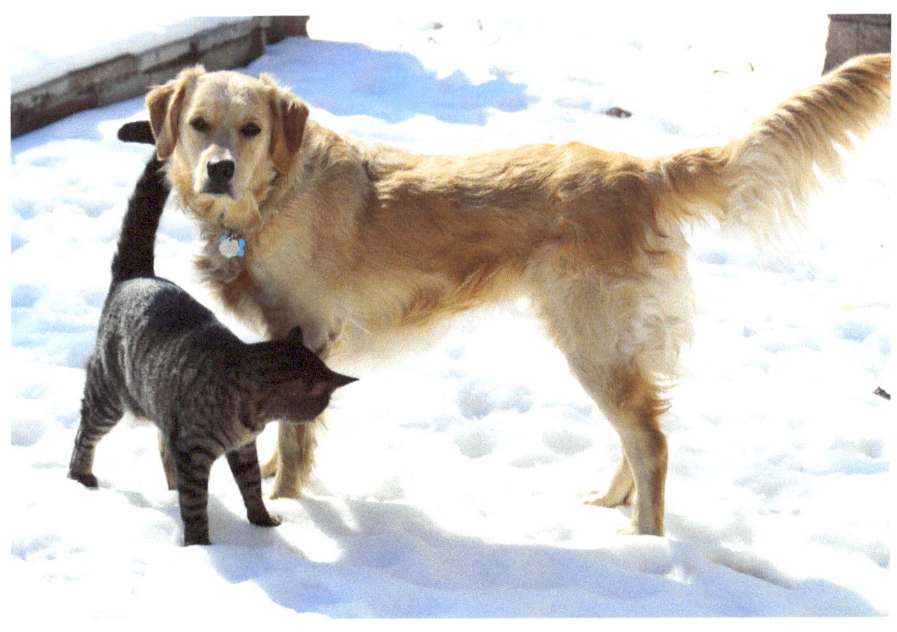

When we are out for a stroll in the park, Joy routinely looks for retaining walls on which to walk. She feels the need to sit up high on any and all benches, tables, and chairs as well. How boring to just walk on a path!

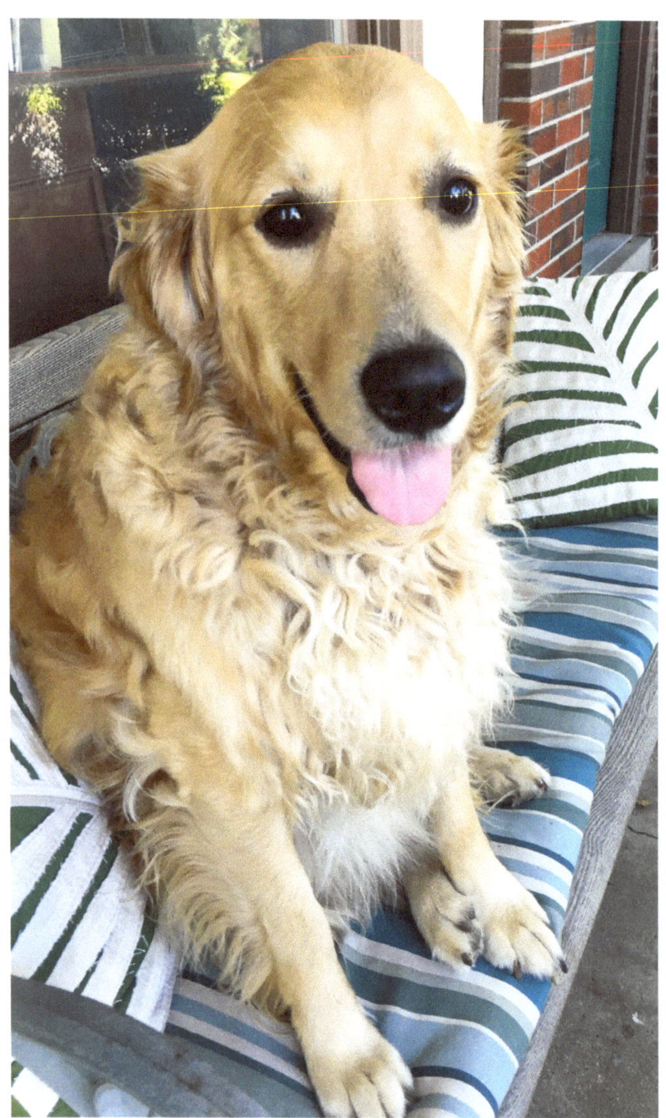

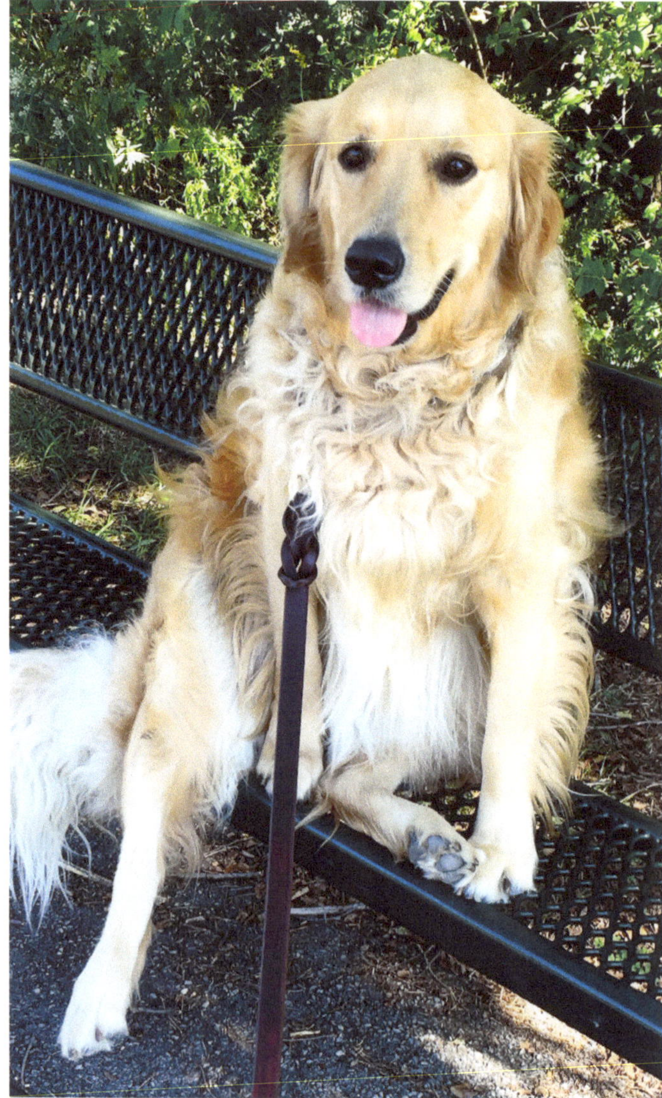

When one of her zillion tennis balls rolled under the TV, I attempted to retrieve it for her. In the process I found a long-lost, large chew bone. I pulled it out and showed it to her. She was amazed! Her face said, "Wow! Mom is a magician! She turned my ball into a bone!

One day as I was sitting at my desk, Joy came and put her feet on the arm of the chair and touched my head with her foot. (She always uses her feet as hands.) I said, "Do you need to go out again?" (She had just been outside!)

She wagged and wagged, so I got up and went to the back door with her. When I opened the door, in came Hunter. Oops! I had forgotten him! Even though it was a very cold, blustery day, I had allowed Hunter go out an hour before because he had insisted. He had probably been sitting at the door meowing to come in out of the cold, but I didn't hear him. But Joy did! So she came to get the help he needed. What a team!

Speaking of teamwork – It's funny to see Joy and Hunter "double-timing" the squirrels as they race away from the bird feeder and head for the woods. Hunter takes the retaining wall route and Joy heads diagonally across the yard to the gate. They never catch the squirrels, but they give them a good run for their money!

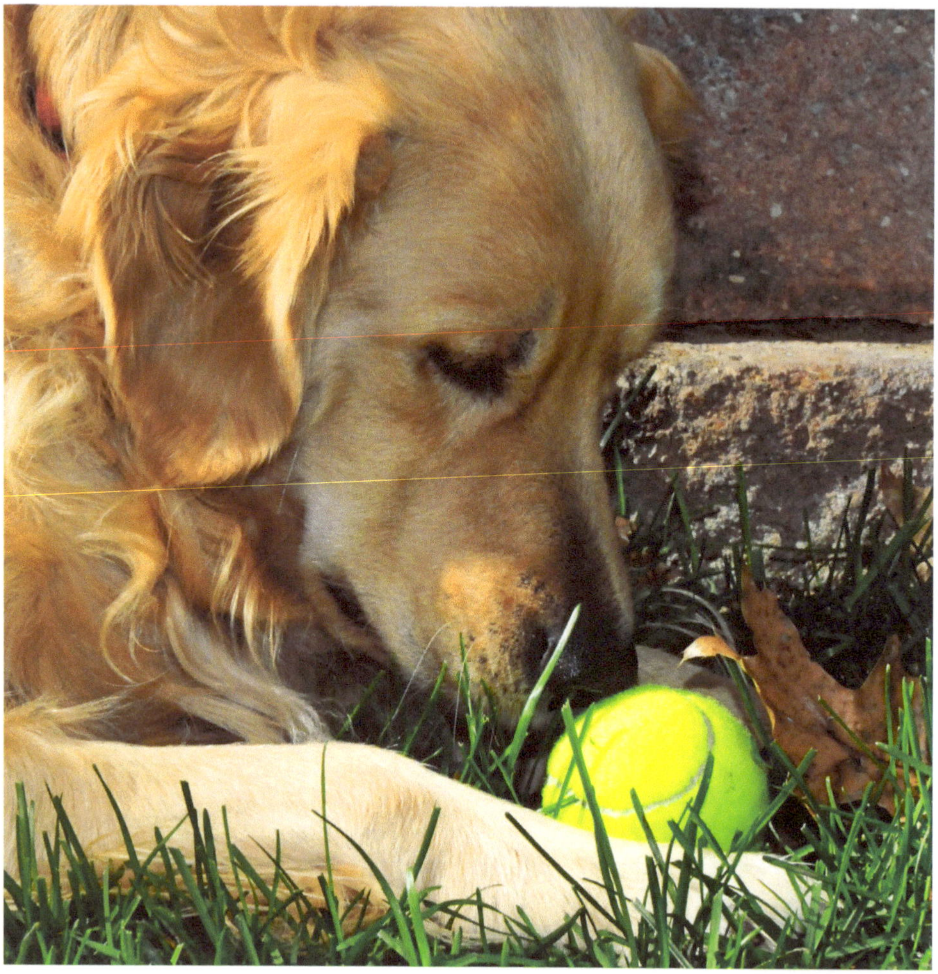

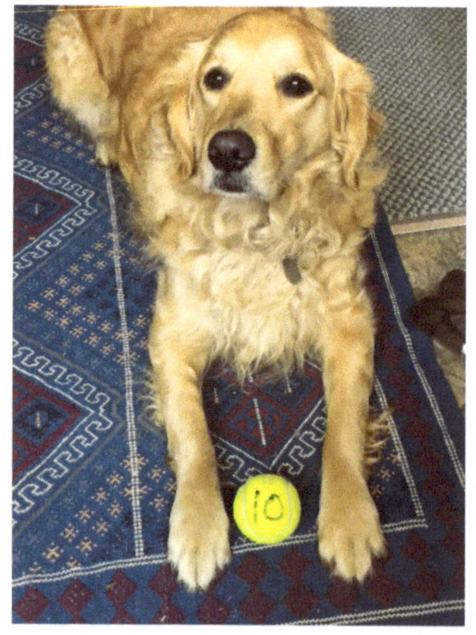
10

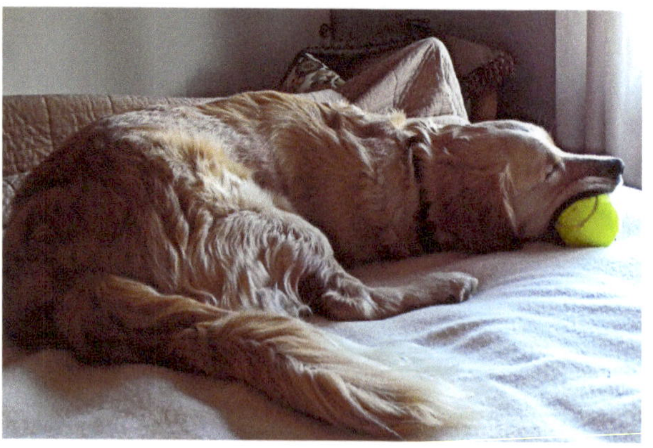

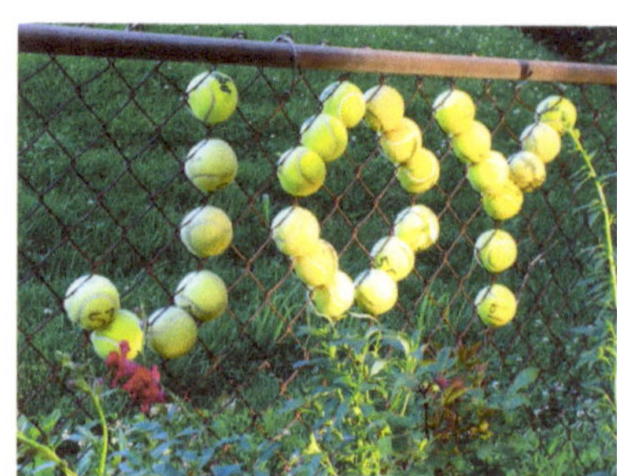
JOY

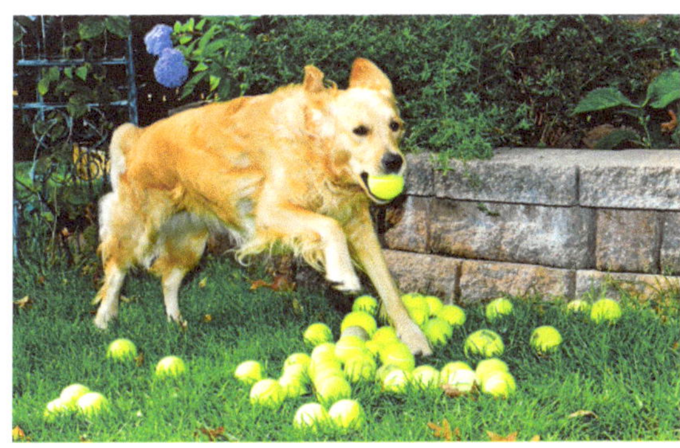

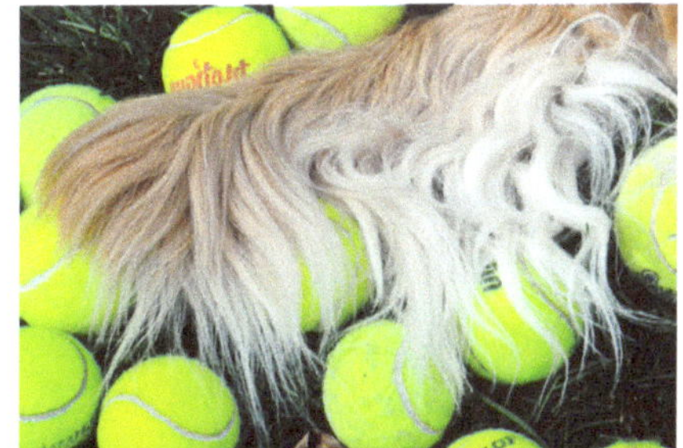

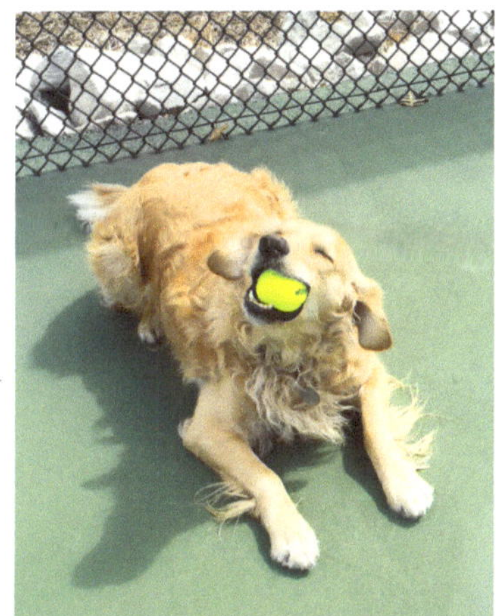

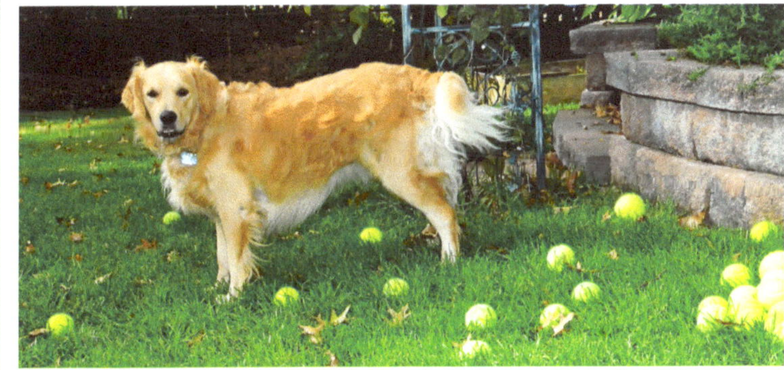

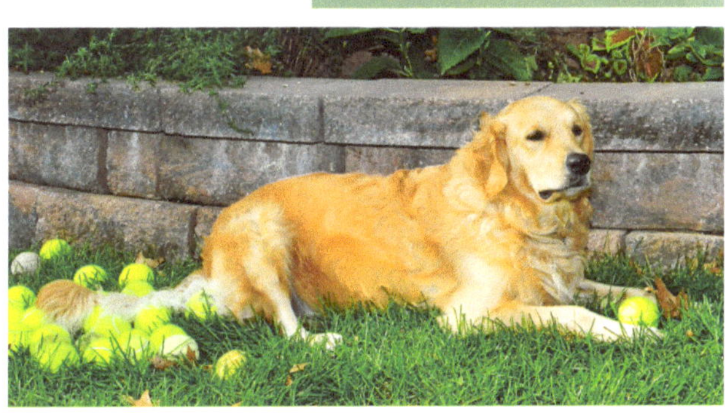

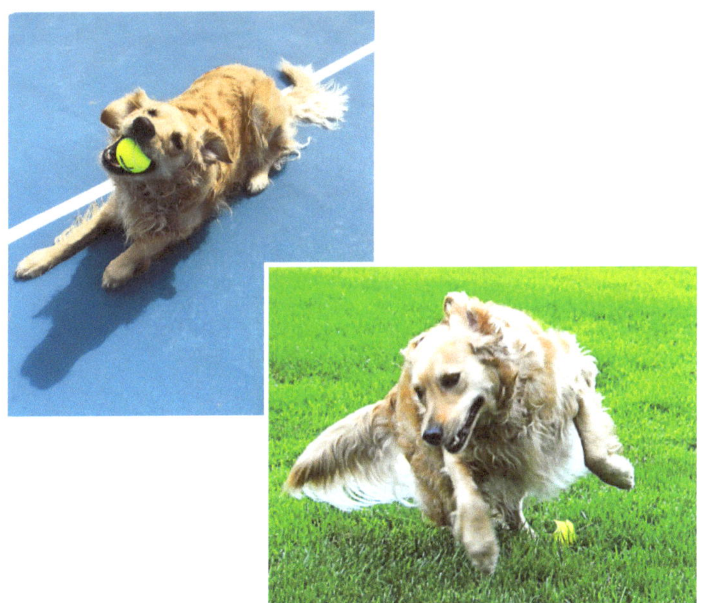

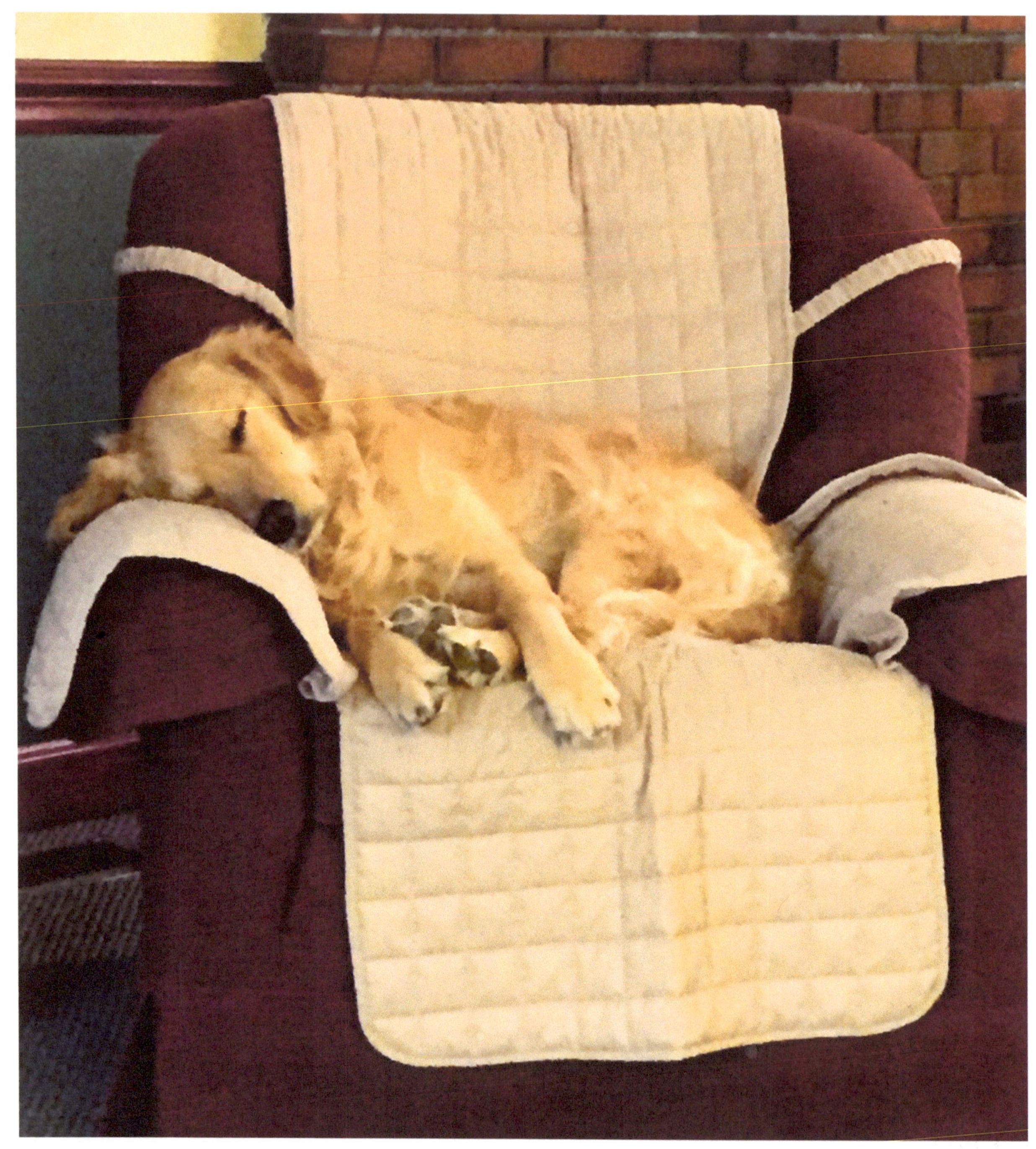

Sleepy puppy

When we found Joy, I knew immediately that the name we'd chosen for her described her perfectly. But it did not occur to me that I would be speaking her name, "Joy," dozens of times each day. And I had no idea that this repetition of the word "joy" would cause me to think about the concept of joy in ways I had never considered.

In the simple, ancient act of "naming," the stage was being set to teach us some lessons about His joy.

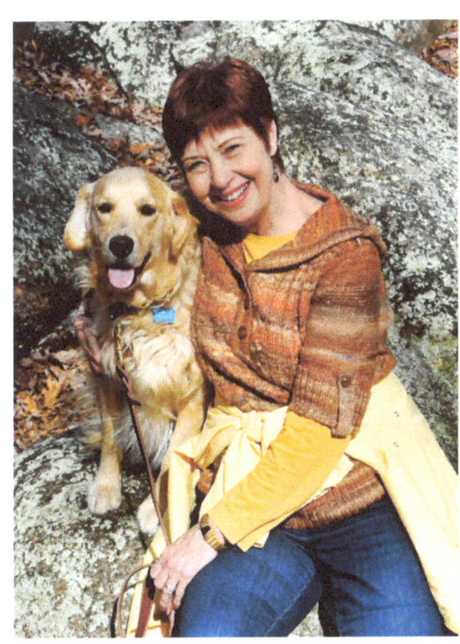

My first outing with Joy.

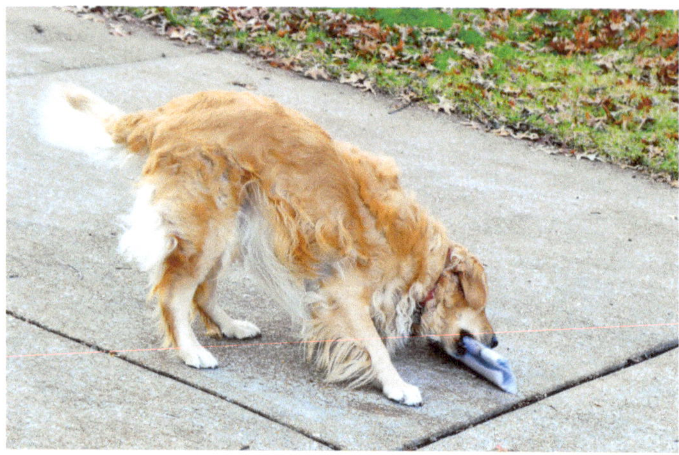

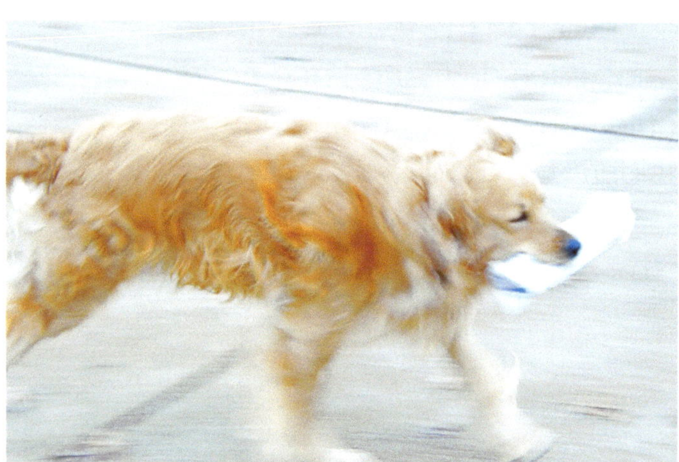

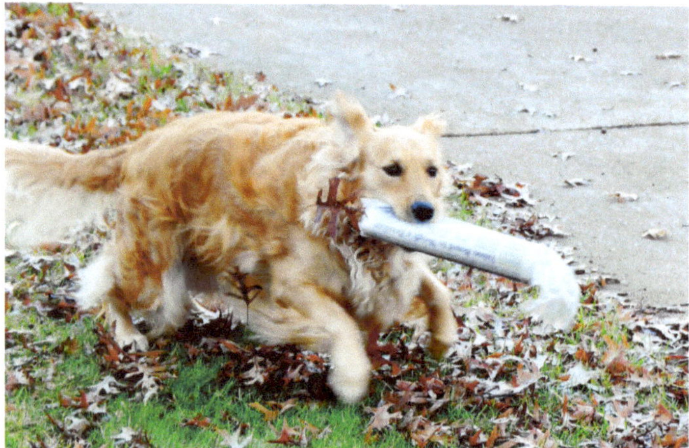

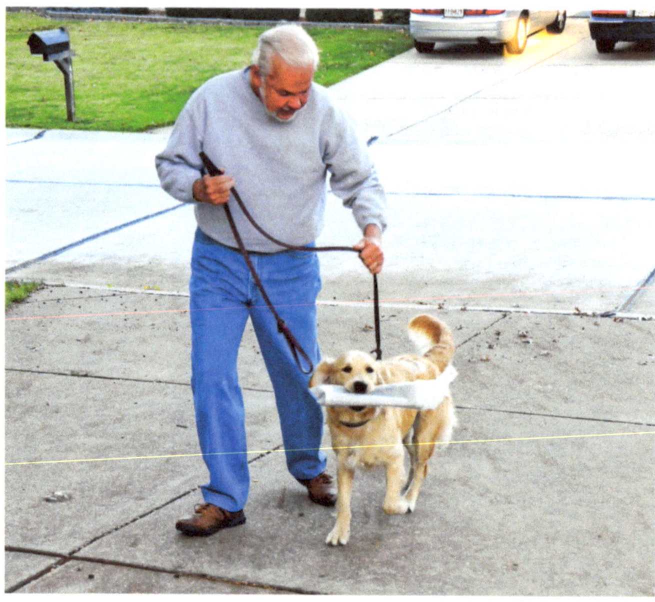

Joy is learning to do her job.

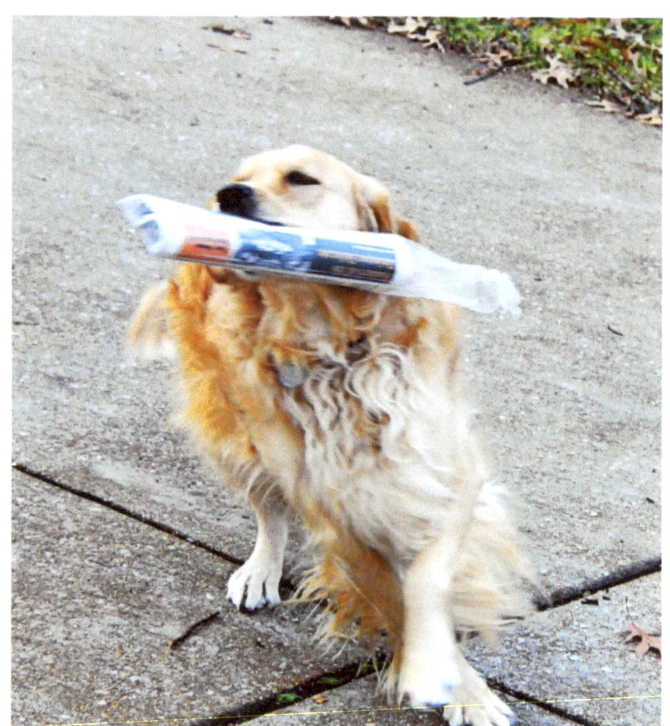

Joy is a Purpose

Each day, Joy is eager for three things – her breakfast, her walk, and her JOB.

Her job? What is her job?

Every morning, Joy goes out to retrieve the morning newspaper for us from the front yard. Rain, snow, sleet or ice – Joy doesn't just "go" out, she "bounds" out!

So if you are one of the people driving up the street while Joy is retrieving the newspaper, you will see her bouncing, dancing, wagging, prancing, and high-stepping. Not only does she pick up the paper, but she tosses it into the air with a flourish, catches it, and then turns to run into the house for her reward – a goodie.

Now why do you think she is so filled with joy? I think it is because in doing her "work," she is doing exactly what she was intended to do, and being exactly what she was intended to be - a Golden RETRIEVER. It is her nature, her birthright from her Creator.

She "retrieves" lots of things. She cannot allow you to return home without greeting you with a toy in her mouth that she "retrieved" for you when she heard the garage door opening. Retrieving is her purpose.

And isn't it just the same with us? We also are filled with joy when we do what we were called to do.

"For we are God's handiwork, created in Christ Jesus to do good works, which God prepared in advance for us to do."

Ephesians 2:10

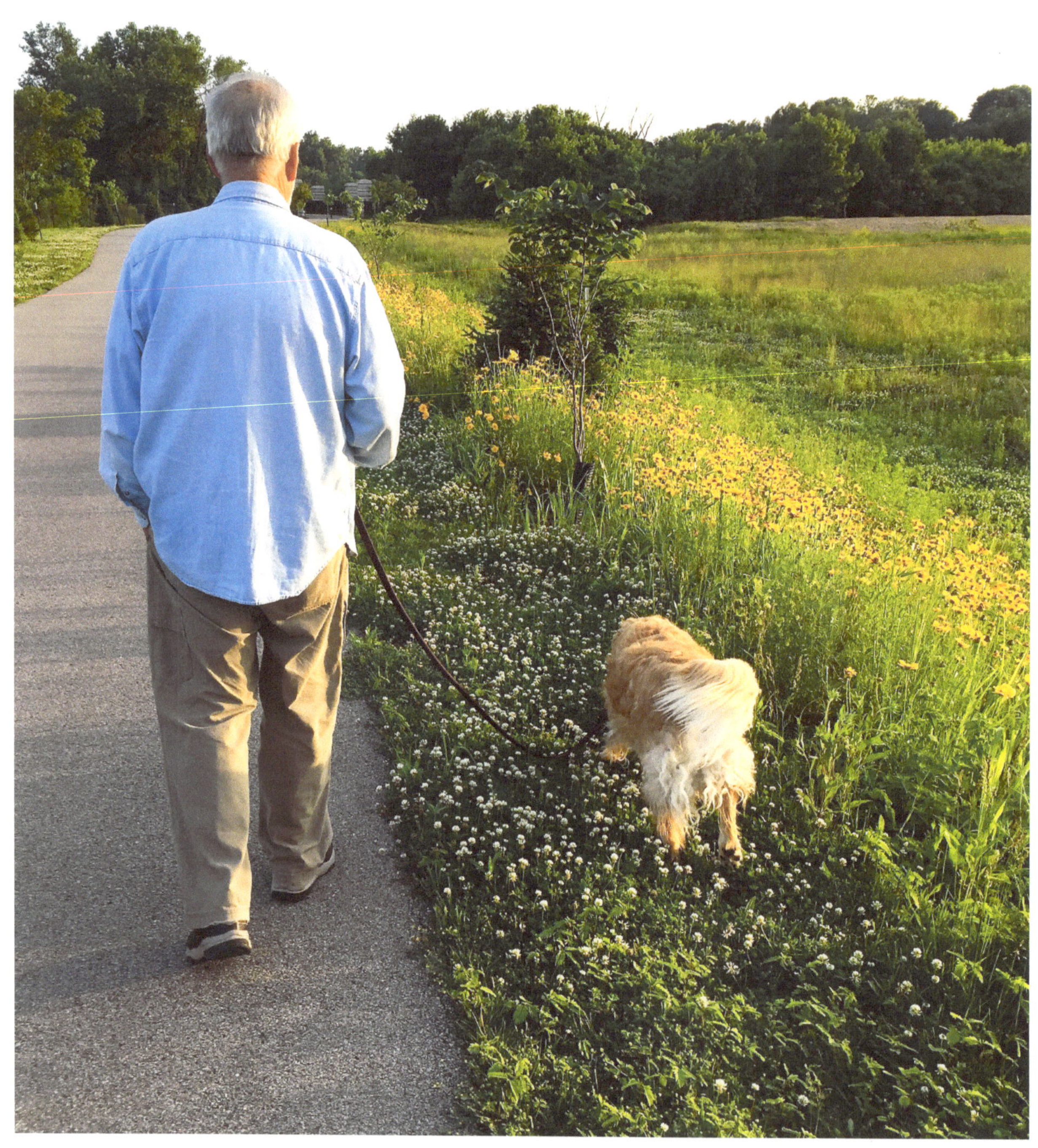

What a joy to go walking with your best friend.

Joy is a Relationship

There are some brand new tennis courts just up the street from our house near a school. Almost every day, Joy and her Daddy take a walk to the schoolyard.

One day, Joy found a lost tennis ball in the grass.

She picked it up, and since nobody else claimed it, she proudly carried it home with an especially high wag in her tail. Daddy praised her. Well-done Joy!

What began as a single incident soon became Joy's quest! Joy has found hundreds of tennis balls . . . really! (Her record number for 2015 was 202 balls!)

Not only is she thrilled by the discovery of the lost balls in high weeds, but Joy is not experiencing this quest alone.

She is delighted in the close companionship of her Daddy, and she is so excited about pleasing me as she comes home through our back gate to find me waiting on the patio. Joys takes a flying leap off the retaining wall and races across the yard to drop the sacred ball at my feet.

It makes me SO happy! And she knows it!

What Joy was first doing by nature now has become a way of pleasing the ones she loves. Now she is no longer just walking aimlessly. Now she is making us happy with her abilities and her gift!

We also are filled with joy when we are walking closely with our Creator and Maker, our Abba Father.

"You have made known to me the paths of life; you will fill me with joy in your presence."

Acts 2:28

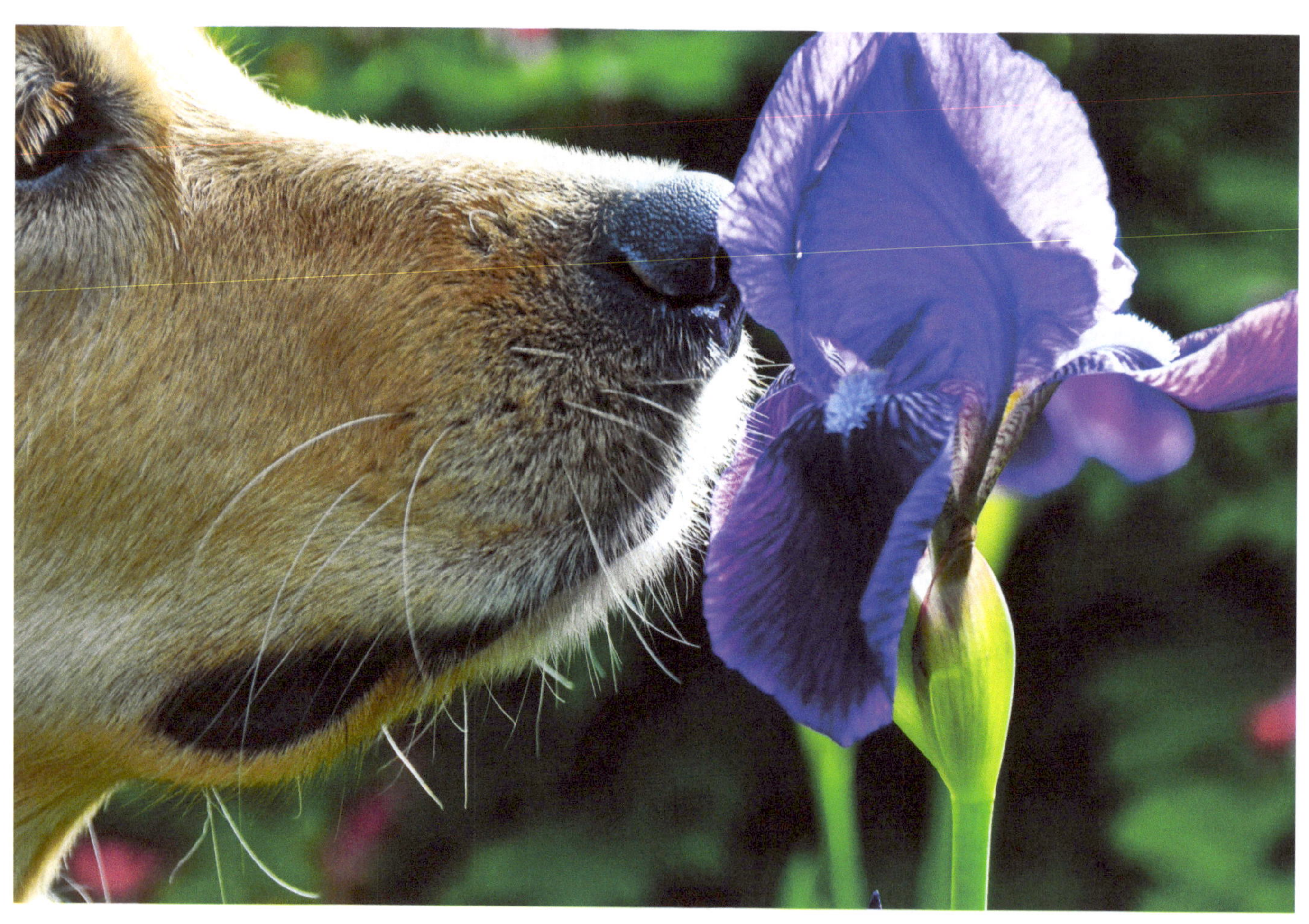

Joy stops to smell the flowers.

Joy is a Choice

Shortly before choosing Joy, I was introduced to a book that presented a simple and profound challenge. *One Thousand Gifts,* by Ann Voskamp, challenged me to take up my pen and paper and to write down the blessings in my life. That simple practice has made me a detective-of-blessings! Though I have not reached the one thousand mark yet, I have written hundreds and hundreds of entries. In no particular order, here are just a few:

298. Joy digging in the sand and burying her toys
299. Quiet Tuesday morning at home
304. Invitation to Thanksgiving dinner
308. Sounds of train whistle
315. One red maple leaf stuck to rain-wet window
273. Surprised by Joy! 10-19-13

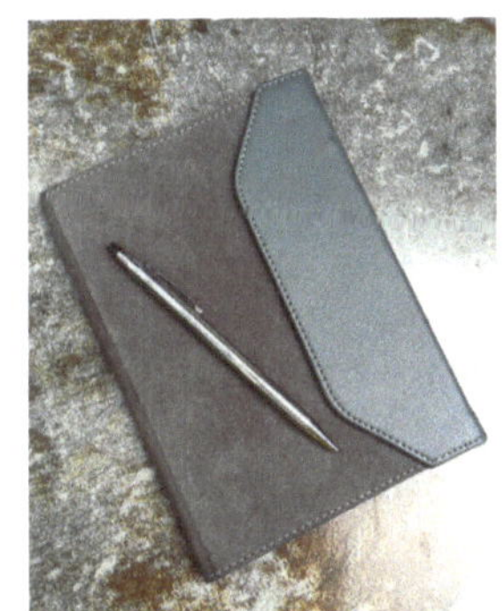

Each gift causes me to give thanks. And in that thankfulness I find great joy. Joy is a result of thanksgiving.

Even just the act of re-reading the blessings I have written down brings back the joy of each of these small gifts and I am thankful again! Had I not written them down, I would have hurried past the original gifts and forgotten about them in seconds.

Once I started the practice and habit of writing down the gifts in my life, I noticed something gradually happening. I started actively looking for the gifts! Because the truth is, the more you are looking, the more you see!

And so I return to that beautiful October day and our first encounter with Joy.

We had a plan all worked out in our minds. We thought we knew how the future was going to look in our home. And yet, in spite of what we thought we wanted and in spite of what we had planned, there was another path for us.

Joy was there . . . right in front of our eyes.

We are so glad that we didn't miss her!

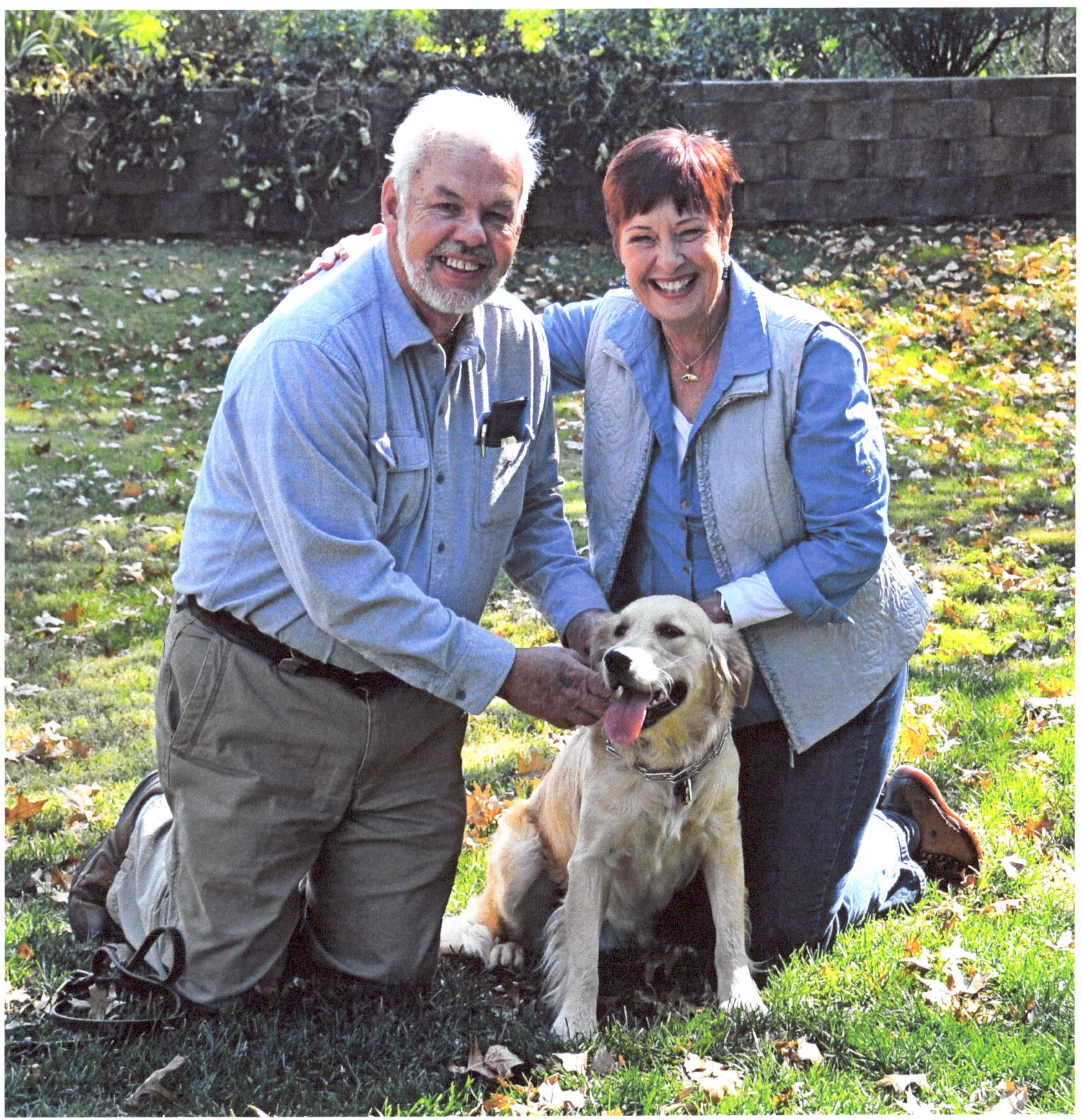

Words of Joy

Would it surprise you to learn that there are 252 occurrences of the word "JOY" in the Bible? Here are a few of my favorite scriptures of joy:

The fruit of the Spirit is love, JOY, peace, patience, kindness, goodness, faithfulness, gentleness, and self-control.

Galatians 5:22

Do not grieve, for the JOY of the Lord is your strength.

Nehemiah 8:10

Do not be afraid. I bring you good news of great JOY that will be for all the people.

Luke 2: 10

You have made known to me the paths of life:
You will fill me with JOY in your presence.

Psalm 16:11

You turned my wailing into dancing; you removed my sackcloth and clothed me with JOY.

Psalm 30:11

Restore to me the JOY of your salvation and grant me a willing spirit, to sustain me.

Psalm 51:12

The meadows are covered with flocks and the valleys are mantled with grain; they shout for JOY and sing.

Psalm 65:13

Satisfy us in the morning with your unfailing love, that we may sing for JOY and be glad all our days.

Psalm 90:14

www.ingramcontent.com/pod-product-compliance
Lightning Source LLC
LaVergne TN
LVHW070206110826
845147LV00002B/519
9798888704554